D1068619

MORE MR. CAT

AND A BIT OF AMBER TOO

By George Freedley

Theatre Collections in Libraries and Museums, 1936
(with Rosamond Gilder)

Theatrical Designs from The Baroque Through Neo-classicism, 1940

A History of The Theatre, 1941, revised 1955
(with John Adams Reeves)

Are You Going to Build A Theatre?, 1947 (with Paul Baker)

A History of Modern Drama, 1947 (with Barrett H. Clark)

Simon Lissim, 1949

The Lunts, 1957

Mr. Cat, 1960

Performing Arts Collections of The World, 1961

GEORGE FREEDLEY

MORE MR. CAT
AND A BIT OF AMBER TOO

Drawings by VICTOR J. DOWLING

Foreword by CARL VAN VECHTEN

GRAMERCY PUBLISHING COMPANY
NEW YORK

DEDICATION

To LILLIAN GISH

CONTENTS

Of the making of cat books.

A Letter of Credit to MORE MR. CAT

Of the making of cat books, there seems to be no end: fairy stories and folk tales; historical summaries; books on health and feeding; anthologies;—all appear in regular rotation. There is another kind of book about the cat, considerably rarer and possibly more valuable: the biography of a particular feline, under which category Charles Dudley Warner, Pierre Loti, Beverly Nichols, and Colette have written extraordinarily fine examples. Even I once attempted a short work in this form. The reason these biographies are possibly more valuable is that in writing of one particular cat the author exploits the individuality of that cat, shows how he (or she) differs from all other cats. This is important, because many people, despite the wealth of evidence to the contrary, still believe that all cats are precisely similar, behave in an identical manner with the cat next door. Certainly this is not the truth. Cats differ as profoundly as men. One cat enjoys a bath; another has a dread of water. One cat prefers fish; another will only eat raw beef; while a third is sufficiently catholic in his taste to partake sometimes of beer and olives. Most cats are abnormally clean but occasionally you will find one with slovenly habits. There are cats who enjoy being brushed; others who hate this manner of torture. I once knew a cat who took pleasure in being dangled by his tail (his name was Croquet, and he lived with Armina Marshall); most other cats would resent this indignity bitterly. Many cats love to chase after mice; but some don't. Few cats eat ·their mice; but some do. The average mother is attentive to her kittens; but I have known mothers who neglect their offspring with authority. Many cats love attention and purr loudly when they sit in a human lap; some dislike attention and remain aloof. Individual cats are aloof and dislike attention; others are attracted by strangers and even show them affection; many pusses slink under the bed when visitors appear.

Mr. Freedley, in his biography of Mr. Cat, added another individual cat to the series of personal portraits. His first book having enjoyed a success, both here and in London, he has written another along similar lines, telling about other cats of his acquaintance, and recalling further incidents in the history of Mr. Cat. Cat lovers will wish him well, and his book *Bon Voyage*.

CARL VAN VECHTEN
New York, April 22, 1962

My first was called Mother Kitty . . . Mr. Cat was Number Thirty-One.

CATS I HAVE KNOWN

I cannot remember a time when there weren't cats about me. My first was called Mother Kitty, a most appropriate name, for she regularly presented us with three or four litters a year. Mother Kitty was an immaculate, short-haired white cat with what must have been an especially vivid red tongue and rosy pads on her paws, because I can still recall them. Her litters, though, were always of widely assorted colors, something which I never quite understood at that time.

What an enormous amount of washing was required to achieve Mother Kitty's perfection! She took care of most of it herself, although there was always the weekly ritual bath which my mother or governess performed, either together or separately. I was allowed to watch and to hand up the bar of Fairy Soap when it was needed, and to hold the extra towels for drying. The best part for me came when Mother Kitty had been dried until her fur was like an aura around her and she was ready to be wrapped in a fresh, dry towel and put in her basket near the open fire in the upstairs sitting room. She purred contentedly while Mother and Edith and I had tea (mine of course was the cambric variety, but it made me feel very grown up indeed). Mother Kitty purred herself to sleep by the fire.

At kitten times, which were more often than not, we would sit on or near the window seat in the bow window facing Lee Circle on Monument Avenue in Richmond, where I was born. Mother Kitty would lounge on the window seat, jumping down every now and then to make sure that her kittens were secure in their basket near our feet. If one of them was picked up to be petted, she would stand guard beside the chair and when she thought the admirer had held the kitten long enough, she'd place a warning paw on the knee. If that were not heeded, her claws would come out lightly, just enough to indicate that she meant business and was not fooling.

I was never myself allowed in on the birthing. *That* took place in a woodshed at the rear of the garden. (In fact I did not become an obstetrical assistant until some fifty years later, when Princess Amber had her first kittens on the kitchen floor the house because my parents had been taught a hard lesson of *St. George and the Dragon* on Fire Island two days after the hurricane of 1960.)

Mother Kitty was allowed to have her kittens with her in by another family cat a few years before my birth. Dandy, a calico, had *not* been allowed to bring her kittens inside though she would fetch them often enough one by one up to the kitchen door. They were unceremoniously sent back to the shed, as of course they were still unhousebroken. My mother and father were newlyweds then and not so wise in the ways of cats as they later came to be. Dandy did not like the woodshed at all. She hated being deprived of her human company, something which felinophobes deny because they do not understand that cats show their affection in subtler fashion than dogs. Dandy reasoned that she was being banished because of the kittens, and, to my parents' horror, she calmly destroyed them.

Through the years from Mother Kitty on, there were always

cats in my life, sometimes two or three, but always at least one. I count in my memory thirty before the one arrived whose name adorns this book.

My mother had always loved cats, going back to her own childhood when she would visit her grandparents on their farm in western New York State. In those days country cats were tolerated only briefly in the kitchen, and the run of the house was strictly denied. Cats were barn animals and were supposed to realize it. Mother thought otherwise, and when she went there to visit and the time came to put the cats out of the kitchen, there was never one in sight. Eventually, her grandparents found out what was happening. They would go to Mother's room to find her sleeping quietly. They would lift the covers carefully so as not to waken her, and find all the cats ranged asleep on either side of her and at her feet, sometimes as many as seven in all. They were removed ever so quietly. Once, though, they woke her up, and she told me that she screamed, "I want my kitties. Give me back my kitties!" until they were restored.

When I was about ten years old we acquired a Maltese male. I know it is fashionable, as Victor Dowling wrote, to refer to them now as short-haired blues, but it was Maltese then. Chin-Chin was the most talkative cat I have ever known, and his name certainly came to him naturally. I remember my father's once making a set of paper booties for Chin-Chin to wear. The outraged cat tore them off, growling indignantly, to our amusement, and then he swatted Father across the hand with claws bared so that *that* experiment was never repeated.

During our summers at Cape May, we lived next door to a handsome Orange Angora (another name no longer in fashion) who lived to over twenty-five, although I never saw him after he reached twenty. I had always wanted to have one of his kittens, and the excitement was tremendous one day when a telegram arrived in Richmond announcing that an orange kitten was en route via Railway Express. I read the wire aloud to Chin-Chin, who seemed distinctly unimpressed.

The day arrived and a yowling wicker basket was brought into the guest room to be opened. I waited anxiously; Chin-Chin warily. When the hamper was opened, despite parental warning I picked out a three-months-old ball of orange fur and cuddled him to stop his yowling. Terrified, he drenched me, a reaction I have never forgotten. (In fact, I remember all too clearly my trepidation years later when the lady from across the hall at East 55th Street reached into a carton to pick up and christen Mr. Cat, whom I was then first bringing home. But Mr. Cat was more polite than my Orange.)

While I was thus being greeted by the new arrival, Chin-Chin, terrified, had let out a matching yowl of his own and fled under a near-by bed, maintaining a three day self-imposed exile except for brief appearances when he would emerge for his dinner or for some other physical necessity.

Chin-Chin conquered his fear of the strange kitten and came to treat him like a favored younger brother and to teach him the ropes of the Freedley household. For obvious reasons our new kitten was named "Trouble," and he was affectionately called that during his long life.

The most exciting thing that ever happened in Trouble's or Chin-Chin's life came when the little Orange Angora was still a kitten and our Maltese was about a year and a half old. We had sold our house on Monument Avenue by then and had taken an apartment around the corner in a six-tenant house on Park Avenue. One evening, when the members of the families were seated on the front terrace which they shared, the two Freedley cats were out chasing Junebugs under the acetylene street lamp. Chin-Chin tired of this game and withdrew to the sidewalk, where he could still keep an eye on his brother. Suddenly, the people gathered on the terrace saw an automobile round the corner at high speed and head up the street directly toward Trouble. Chin-Chin dashed to the kitten, batting him rapidly with extended front paw, and pushed him to the curb, placing his own body between Trouble and the oncoming car.

The driver passed without ever realizing what had happened. Chin-Chin and Trouble came racing back across the street to be examined and exclaimed over and wondered at by their awe-struck owners and friends. Two witnesses were present during this experience who swore they had never been cat lovers up to this point and would never have believed the story if they had not been there themselves. If there was ever a feline David and Jonathan relationship this was it, although we refrained from changing our cats' names.

The personalities of my other cats blur in my memory during the years when I was away at college or later when I went North to Yale Drama School, an institution which did not encourage its graduate students to keep cats. (Perhaps Yale has learned better by now.) However, I do remember number thirty very well indeed. She was a dainty Maltese named Dinah, whom we acquired shortly after moving to Briarcliff Manor in New York State, a few months before Pearl Harbor.

Dinah was a lively and affectionate cat who was a house pet but could be counted on to keep the vagrant rodent population under control. During the week she slept on a settee at the foot of my parents' bed, and on cold nights she crept closer for warmth and companionship. On Friday nights, when I would arrive to spend the weekend, she switched her allegiance and moved to my bed, curling in the crook of my left arm and purring herself and me to sleep.

Dinah was a charming companion, and there was never anything unhappy in her life until the day two years after her arrival when she was struck by a passing automobile and killed almost before our eyes. Not wanting to make myself vulnerable to such hurt again, I went on a cat strike which lasted until August 2nd, 1943, when I first laid eyes on Mr. Cat and knew that we were meant to be together.

2

MR. CAT AND THE ELECTRIC EYE

The block in East 55th Street between Madison and Fifth Avenues where Mr. Cat and I were living during the war was primarily made up of brownstone houses built in the mid-nineteenth century as private homes and later converted to apartment houses with shops at street level. 711 Fifth Avenue still stands on the north corner opposite the impressive St. Regis Hotel which dominates the block. Four and five story buildings occupied the rest of both sides of the street.

West of us is a brownstone which, during Prohibition, housed on its top floor a small and delightful speakeasy, much frequented by theatrical folk who enjoyed its intimacy and its small terraces, front and back. By the time in 1943 that Mr. Cat had come to live with me, drinking had become legal once again, the speakeasy had gone with Repeal and a young architect had taken over the flat and reconstructed it with many modern devices.

About 1946, Mr. Cat discovered this rendezvous on one of his nocturnal prowls. He was still allowed out at that time to roam the maze of fire escapes and roof tops, for we knew that there was no exit to the street except through shops or restaurants. I learned of Mr. Cat's discovery of this apartment when I received a telephone call at the Library early one morning. "Are you the George Freedley who lives in 55th Street and owns a big Persian cat?"

"Yes," I said, wondering what was in store.

"Well, I nearly shot that cat last night!"

"What!" I gasped.

"If I had a gun I would have shot him," the angry voice continued. "And if I could have caught him I would have wrung his neck."

"Who is this?" I asked.

It was, of course, the young architect, who went on. "I live on the top floor just west of you and for the past three nights around four o'clock in the morning your blasted cat has come into my apartment and run all over the place opening the doors and turning on the lights!"

Now everyone had conceded that Mr. Cat was very intelligent and quite clever, but this accomplishment seemed beyond even his talents.

"Would you please try to be more coherent," I asked. "I think I've missed something somewhere."

My caller took a deep breath and began in a more conversational tone to explain that the doors of his apartment worked on electric beams. The door opened when the beam was broken, and, when they opened, the lights in the next room were turned on automatically. "And," he continued, "your cat can break the beam when his tail is straight up in the air, and everything starts working. I've had to get up to chase him out of the apartment. I can't catch him, he's too fast and for his sake it's good he's fast."

I had to cover the phone with my hand so my caller would not hear my laughter as I pictured the sleepy and stumbling man pursuing Mr. Cat in full flight as doors opened and closed and lights flashed on and off. I controlled my

When his tail is straight up in the air.

laughter enough to apologize and to ask what I could do to remedy the situation.

By this time, the gentleman had calmed down. "I don't mean to be unreasonable," he said, "But I do think I have a right to sleep the night through without being disturbed by these visits at such an ungodly hour. I do love animals and I wouldn't mind his coming in any time after eight in the morning and before eleven at night, but I do think he should be kept home between those hours. I admit I probably won't shoot him, but I will have to do something if he continues."

I promised that I would take action immediately, and that our neighbor could retire with assurance that he would not be visited at night. I knew this was no time to antagonize him by suggesting that he open his windows at the top instead of at the bottom, in case he had already tried that and the agile and acrobatic Mr. Cat had surmounted that difficulty.

It was this measure I took at home. It was mid-winter, so opening the window at the top only an inch or two provided enough ventilation for humans while prohibiting prowling pussy cats from getting out.

Horace Smith, the superintendent of my apartment house, asked how I had made out with our neighbor. It was he who had told him whom to call concerning the visiting cat. He also reminded me of the tenant on the third floor who had screened her windows after Mr. Cat had made a few midnight leaps from the fire escape to the middle of her bed. Horace thought that would be an excellent solution to our neighbor's problem, but I thought it wiser not to suggest it in the strained circumstances.

Mr. Cat did not like the curfew, but he accepted it grudgingly. He made a nightly inspection of all the windows in the apartment in the hope that one might have been left open by mistake, then would return with a plop of resignation to the foot of my bed.

A few months passed. Spring came, then summer and then a heat wave. The windows had to be opened and out went Mr. Cat. I was apprehensive at first and answered each telephone call nervously, but there was no worrying word from the gadget lover until the Sunday evening when I arrived home about ten-thirty to a rousing feline welcome and a ringing phone. Mr. Cat and I went to answer it. He jumped up on the Thomas Jefferson designed desk in my bedroom on which the phone sat, as I picked up the receiver. It was that man's voice, "Have you seen your cat tonight?"

"Why, yes," I answered nervously, "He's right here. Why?"

"Have you looked at him carefully? Does he look different?"

I reached out to Mr. Cat and turned him over on his back, but there was nothing different I could see which fact I reported to my caller.

"What about his identification tag?" he asked.

I looked at Mr. Cat's harness. There was no tag. It was gone.

"I just came home a few minutes ago," said my neighbor, "and guess what I found right in the middle of my living room floor."

I gave Mr. Cat a dirty look. He had all the back alley to roam and he had to pick that particular spot, of all places, to leave a calling card. I attempted a slightly confused explanation that since the weather had turned hot and since there had been no trouble for months, I thought Mr. Cat might have forgotten about the intriguing devices that had fascinated him earlier.

"He *has* been very good," said the young man. "I'm not calling to complain. I haven't seen him at all if he has been coming in and I never would have discovered it if I hadn't found the tag. I'd just like to get it back to him."

I was naturally much relieved at the change in his attitude and offered to go and fetch the tag but thought perhaps the gentleman might like to come over for a drink and meet Mr. Cat on his own home grounds. The invitation was accepted and the young man soon appeared with the incriminating evidence. Mr. Cat was politely formal and gave no indication that he had ever seen this person before.

Undoubtedly it was that friendly acquaintance as much as humanity that led the young man to call me a few months later to say he had acquired two dogs, dachshunds that would pass easily under the light beams without breaking the connection, and that Mr. Cat should be careful. Whether Mr. Cat overheard the conversation or just naturally caught the scent of the new tenants while prowling about is uncertain, but that apartment was stricken from that time on from his visiting list.

3

MR. CAT IS CAUGHT IN A SHOP WINDOW, AND SO AM I

Until he was allowed out no longer, Mr. Cat used to visit the work room of one of the dress shops located on the street floor of the building where I live. I only assumed this and did not come to feel reasonably sure of it until the night the Theatre Guild held a gala cebration, show and supper dance at the Hotel Plaza in honor of the third of *Oklahoma!*'s continuous years on Broadway and the completion of the first year for *Carousel*.

Shortly before three A.M., Dorothy Kneeland, a willowy Maryland-born blonde buyer for Lord and Taylor, and my date for the evening, decided we had had enough of the party and would go back to my apartment for a post-mortem drink. We left Ed Burke, who shares the apartment, dancing with an energetic redhead.

The Spring evening was balmy so Dotty and I walked slowly down Fifth Avenue to 55th Street and up to the apartment where Mr. Cat greeted us. Dotty played with him while I mixed drinks, but when we settled down to our discussion of who was or was not at the party, and the comparison of this with other similar affairs, Mr. Cat slipped out quietly, bored with a conversation which had no interest for him.

About half an hour later we were startled by the headlong entrance of Mr. Cat. He rushed to the far end of the living room, opposite the entrance door, then flung himself down, curled up and pretended to be fast asleep.

A moment or two later we heard the elevator arrive, and Ed burst in the front door. He stopped amazed when he saw Mr. Cat stretched out, fast asleep.

"What are you doing here?" he asked. "How did you get up here so quickly?"

Mr. Cat blinked lazily at him and then curled up in a tighter ball, registering annoyance at having his rest disturbed.

Ed turned to us, "When did he come in?"

We answered that he had come charging in only a moment before and asked why it was important.

"Well," said Ed, "as I came along the street I saw two couples standing in front of the dress shop window. They were knocking on the window and laughing and obviously fascinated with something going on inside. I peered over their shoulders to look in the shop. And there was Himself, posing and preening between two Paris originals. Then he sauntered over and pretended to sniff at the fingers one of the girls was

Mr. Cat registers annoyance.

running up and down the window. I moved to one side and he looked up and saw me."

" 'You!' I said and pointed my finger right at him, 'What are you doing here!' He did the most wonderful double take I've ever seen. He blinked, shook his head, dropped open his jaw, and stared again as if he couldn't believe his eyes. Then he cleared out of that window in one jump and took off like a shot. He must have broken every fire escape climbing record getting up here."

I went over to Mr. Cat. "Look," I said, "there's no use pretending. You got caught. You know what you did was bad. Suppose it were the owner and not Ed who found you in the window. Then there'd be real trouble." I was answered with a look of complete innocence and complete puzzlement as to what I was talking about. Dotty burst into laughter at his act and Ed and I joined in. This was definitely disconcerting. No cat likes to be laughed at. He rose and marched indignantly from the room. I heard him jump up on my bed. Obviously the fun for the evening was over.

Mr. Cat will be inevitably linked in my mind with another 55th Street spot, though he never was a visitor or patron there so far as I know. This is L'Aiglon, a popular French dining place in our block. In the late forties and early fifties this restaurant featured a man-made waterfall at its north end. Later, when some patrons complained that the incessant sound of falling water made them "nervous," the cascade was removed, although it was beautiful and refreshing to behold on a warm day.

On the occasion of Mr. Cat's first unexplained absence from home, I went up and down the fire escapes and over the low roofs looking for him and calling. I worked my way toward Fifth Avenue and eventually found my progress blocked by a projection. Originally this must have been a bow window when the building was a residence. A narrow vertical shutter stood open and I thought that this could have intrigued any feline on the prowl.

I stepped around the shutter to see where the opening might lead. I realized my mistake instantly when a second step took me directly beneath the waterfall and I saw the full restaurant through the curtain of falling water. Instinctively I stepped back to put myself out of sight, but just at that instant my eyes met and held those of a lady lunching with another woman at a side table. Though I never went back to explain, I have often imagined the conversation between the ladies right after the incident:

"I just saw a man behind the waterfall."

"Don't be silly. How could there be a man behind the waterfall?"

"But there was. I know. He looked right at me."

"My dear, are you sure you feel all right. You did have a second martini." . . .

To that unfortunate lady who has gone through the years thinking she had an hallucination, I can now offer proof that there *was* a man behind the waterfall. I do hope she reads this and shows it to her skeptical friend.

The advent of a new baby.

4

MR. CAT ATTENDS A SPEECH CLASS

Within Mr. Cat's visiting range, via the fire escapes and back alleys, was the apartment of a well-known acting and speech coach. This lady always welcomed Mr. Cat, by day or night, although with the advent of a new baby in her household she was for a time persuaded to screen her visitor out. The reason for this, she admitted, was that someone had told her that cats will suck a baby's breath at night.

I assured her that this was an old wives' tale, possibly based on the fact that when a baby appears on the premises out of nowhere he is an object of curiosity to any normal cat, something to be smelled and closely inspected. She seemed reassured, and, as the child grew and took matters into its own hands by falling in love with Mr. Cat, the screens were taken down. All the family came to look forward to Mr. Cat's visits.

One time this was not true. One Sunday afternoon my telephone rang, and I heard the well-modulated tones of the speech teacher apologizing for troubling me. "We all do love Mr. Cat," she said, "but at the moment I'm holding a speech class and I'm afraid he's distracting it completely."

"What now?" I thought.

"Could you possibly come and take him home. He won't

come to me and I can't put him out the back way or I wouldn't trouble you."

"Where is he?" I asked, "and what is he doing?"

"Well," she explained, "He's out on the ledge that runs just below our front windows. He must have come in the back window and crossed the apartment and got out without anyone seeing him. He apparently wants to leave, but the sight of all the people in the class, has intimidated him. He appears at one window and seems to be about to leap down and cross the room, but by that time every eye is on him and he backs away. Then he appears at the other window and behaves the same way. *Then* he disappears for three or four minutes and it starts all over again. We've even tried complete silence with everyone sitting still, but he just will not come in. As far as the class is concerned absolutely nothing has been accomplished for the past thirty minutes. And this is the only day they have since they work all week. So could you please come?"

Realizing that this was a matter of time and money as far as both teacher and pupils were concerned, I rushed out of the apartment just stopping long enough to ferret out Mr. Cat's leash, not bothering to change my sports shirt. I rounded Madison Avenue at a clip and soon found the building in 56th Street that housed the harrassed class.

The speech teacher met me at the door and explained further that one of her pupils was the sort completely terrified of cats. The whole episode might have been treated as a joke and the class could have continued as usual but Mr. Cat's erratic appearances made the ailurophobic student a nervous wreck.

She then led me to the front room, which was being used as the class room. She opened the door and I entered. There sat the class formally arranged in a semi-circle of folding chairs. "This then," said all their glances, "is the irresponsible person responsible for that animal."

"Now just where is he?" I asked.

"Right over here," she said, and started across the room to the windows. I followed, and every eye accompanied me. I felt exactly like Clyde Beatty and uttered a silent prayer that this time, if never before or after, Mr. Cat would come immediately when called.

I stuck my head out the window. Mr. Cat was nowhere in sight. The ledge ran along the front of this building and continued along the adjoining building. On the other building's ledge were flower boxes, full of false foliage at this time, very green and very bushy. Trying to put all the assurance I did not feel into my voice I called, "Mr. Cat?"

Immediately the head of Himself poked itself around one of the far flower boxes. There was a look of intense and very pleased surprise in his eyes as they met mine. This was indeed a fine turn and without a moment's hesitation he came along with surefooted determination straight to me. Before he could get over his surprise I snapped the leash on his harness and scooped him up, turning back into the room. The class broke into applause and I must confess I didn't know whether to take a bow or strangle the miscreant for their further entertainment.

5

NURSE CAT

On the occasions when I was ill at home with influenza or colds and once with pneumonia, there was no more attentive and devoted nurse than Mr. Cat. Fred, the late Frederic Brandt, my doctor, always had to move him to the other side of the bed so that he could sit down to examine me. Nurse Cat, as he was referred to during invalid periods, watched with interest the dangling stethoscope, but made no effort to touch it, although it swung perilously near his nose occasionally. When the doctor had finished his examination, he never failed to stroke my companion and whisper instructions in Mr. Cat's ear. This action tickled, and soon a warning paw was raised to the doctor's cheek and he desisted.

After his breakfast, Mr. Cat would hop on the bed and keep vigil until about three in the afternoon by which time I was usually napping and he felt he could go off duty. He then jumped down silently and moved into the living room to curl up on the sofa for a nap of his own free of responsibility.

If I woke up and called him, he would return, otherwise he would content himself with occasional visits, sauntering in at odd times, until proper bedtime.

In 1953 I was taken seriously ill and carted off to the hospital. Mr. Cat had not enjoyed all the activities of doctors and stretcher bearers and was conspicuously restive over my disappearance. He searched the apartment thoroughly each day for a time, then seemed to accept it stoically. The daily reports given him about my condition did not seem to mean much to him.

After six weeks, the daily reports on Mr. Cat were really not enough for me because I missed him so much. I knew animals are forbidden to enter most hospitals for humans, so I said nothing. One evening, about seven-thirty after supper was out of the way, I was doing some casual reading when Ed Burke entered the room, grinning with self-importance and suppressed excitement. He closed the door behind him and as he turned I saw he held Mr. Cat's carrier in one hand. His raincoat was slung casually through the crook of his arm so that it dangled and draped itself over most of the traveling case. Ed crossed the room and set the carrier down on the bed beside me and opened it. Mr. Cat's very surprised face appeared. Ed lifted him into my good arm, and I hugged him as best I could. The sound known as the "purr factory" began at once.

"I wasn't sure I could bring it off," said Ed, "So I didn't prepare you. I was sure I'd be challenged at the elevator or at the desk, but I just swept by them as though it was an ordinary valise I had, and no one even looked twice."

My nurse, the two-legged kind, was not quite sure how to deal with the situation. She had heard so much about Mr. Cat she was delighted to see him in person, but what his presence meant as far as hospital discipline was concerned horrified her. She decided a tactful exit was the best solution, and she left.

Mr. Cat, meanwhile, had passed the period of joyful recognition and had raised his head to view the surroundings with great suspicion. He began to sniff that hospital smell. He

A question of hospital discipline.

didn't like it any better than I did and let out a discomfited
wail. He jumped down from the bed and began to run about
the room, examining every corner and yowling at regular
intervals. I asked to hold him again, so Ed put him back on
the bed. He struggled in my grasp, however, and headed for
his carrier. He clawed at the top, announcing it was time to
go home. He'd had enough of this place. It was obvious he
was a home nurse and that hospitals were not for him. I
hated to see him go, but he had provided the most pleasant
visit of my convalescence.

On the day I was at last released from the hospital, having
learned to walk all over again, a friend came for me and drove
me home. Mr. Cat was waiting at the door and a proper
reunion took place. A week later we were driven to Long
Island to take a boat to Fire Island where I was to spend the
next two months recuperating before I could return to work
at the Library. Since I couldn't manage stairs, a bedroom was
arranged for me on the first floor. Mr. Cat shared this with
me, but sometimes at night I would sense his departure from
the bed for a tour of exploration to make certain that everything on the second story was secure.

Early each morning when I took my short practice walk
I now had company. Always before Mr. Cat was content to go
off about his own business on release each day, but now,
perhaps because my new pace was slow enough to permit an
inquisitive cat time to explore and examine all he wished and
still keep up, Mr. Cat strolled with me. He always managed
to avoid the cane skillfully and sometimes would run a little
ahead to sit and wait, looking back with encouragement, as I
struggled along to catch up. The jaunt would come to an
abrupt conclusion only when some other early riser would
start off for the grocery store dragging his express wagon
behind him. The rattle and bang of this iron monster as it
came along the boardwalk was the signal for Mr. Cat to
disappear into the underbrush.

But when I came home again, Nurse Cat sat awaiting me
at the back door, ready for breakfast.

6

MORE MR. CAT ON FIRE ISLAND

In the summer of 1948 on Fire Island when we rented the two story Dutch colonial cottage from Mrs. Hallye Cannon Clogg, former dancer and later the wardrobe mistress of the Theatre Guild, I carefully explained that Mr. Cat was part of the household.

"Cats I don't mind, and dogs I don't mind," she replied with a twinkle in her clear, blue eyes, "but I draw the line at Shetland ponies." I had heard that the season before Hallye insisted that the oversized and shaggy dog who had lived with former tenants wasn't a dog at all but really a pony.

"I like cats," Hallye continued, "but I like birds, too. I don't like cats chasing birds. Don't let him chase birds."

I promised to do my best, but how can you promise for a cat where birds are concerned? We knew Mr. Cat hated pigeons because when he saw them sail by the windows in town, or come to roost on a near-by window ledge, he grumbled audibly. (That was how I learned my first definite word in cat language, "pigeon." It is difficult to describe and almost impossible to put into phonetics. It is a combination of chattering of the teeth while making a broken gutteral sound rather like a growl, all this while lashing the tail wildly. The latter part, alas, I have been totally unable to approximate. It was on the Island that I discovered the sound meant "pigeon" only, and not "bird" when I saw a thrush land on the porch rail, and I signalled Mr. Cat accordingly. He rushed to the window only to discover that it was *not* a pigeon at all. He gave me a deeply disgusted look and walked away. Obviously his look meant the poor fool can't tell the difference between a bird and a pigeon.)

I will say that in his twelve summers on Fire Island Mr. Cat caught only one bird to my knowledge. Since he brought everything he ever caught back for admiration and praise, I feel sure that this was the only one. And this silly bird brought on its own fate. I discovered a small warbler had managed to get into the screened front porch of the old *St. George and the Dragon.* I carefully propped open the screen door to give him an exit, and tried to shoo him out. The bird simply panicked and swooped from one end of the porch to the other, by-passing the way to safety completely. Deciding that my presence was too exciting, and that at a calm moment it might discover the exit, I left after warning the warbler that a certain cat lived in this house and that it had better leave before that cat came home. I went around to the back steps and settled down with a book to read while awaiting developments. About twenty minutes later I suddenly heard the triumphant call of the successful hunter which announces food for his family. Around the corner of the house came Mr. Cat bringing his trophy. I had to accept the offering. After all, this was not only a bird, but an invader, successfully vanquished.

While truthfully reporting the incident later to our landlady, I learned that she had seen Mr. Cat stalking a bird near our theatre in the Community House. There is a great gap between stalking and catching, and one must remember birds have the added great advantage of flight. When cats learn to fly then birds had better watch out, and so had the rest of us.

Of course, dogs were Mr. Cat's principal enemy, and he would not allow one on his premises. I informed all guests that Mr. Cat was adamant on this point. Once we had attempted a weekend visit with our old friend Polly Dick and her Dandie

Dinmont, Charlie, and it was a time of strain and despair for all concerned. Charlie was confined to the upstairs guest room when Mr. Cat was in the house, and when Nature called the dog, or a run on the beach was planned for him, he had to be smuggled in and out. I would try to distract Mr. Cat, while Polly sauntered down the stairs with a sweater artfully draped over a wriggling Charlie in her arms, and made a dash for the back door and freedom. On Charlie's return, if Mr. Cat were out on a ramble, he was allowed a thorough tour of the house. As a good terrior should, he snuffled every nook and corner getting those indescribable dog thrills from the new animal scent. After his return to the guest room, and Mr. Cat's return to the house, the feline sniffing would begin and Himself suspiciously traced Charlie's progress through his territory. The trail would end at the guest room where Mr. Cat would try to insert himself, nose first, under the crack of the door. In frustration he would clump across the hall to my room, where he would lie with his gaze fastened on that hostile closed door. When the weekend was over we were all relieved.

Mr. Cat on Fire Island.

There was only one occasion upon which Mr. Cat tolerated a dog under his own roof. I have repeatedly heard that all domestic animals understand the function of a seeing-eye dog and never bother those wonderful guides when they are on duty. I was not sure that Mr. Cat shared this forbearing attitude so that when a sightless neighbor arrived for dinner with his German Shepherd companion, I was apprehensive of Mr. Cat's reaction. They had seen each other often while sunning on their respective decks, but this was a definite invasion of territory. Mr. Cat came forward to greet the guests and then he spotted Doe, the guide dog, but instead of leaping forward, hissing, snarling and shrieking, he retreated warily. He backed to a position near the kitchen door and as Doe settled down by her master's chair, Mr. Cat crouched down, peaceful, but wary.

Doe really wanted to make friends as she had known several amiable cats and enjoyed playing with them. Once she was assured her master was settled for a time, she rested her head on her paws with her long nose pointed toward Mr. Cat and made small encouraging sounds of friendship. Mr. Cat, however, had made enough concession and would not relax beyond the point of toleration. Several times, Doe began to inch forward, but Pat, her owner, would catch the sound and warn her back.

They stayed for several hours and when they departed, I sat down to stroke Mr. Cat and congratulate him on his courtesy. He stared solemnly at me and I interpreted his glance to mean that this was to be the one exception; the dispensation was not granted to other dogs. I promised him there would be no others and I kept my word.

I have seen fury on Mr. Cat's face when he was being forcibly put into his carrier about to travel to or from Fire Island. He could become so violent it became necessary to wear heavy leather gloves to guard against scratches. Even these gloves were not proof against his sharp teeth if he chose to bite through in order to effect an escape. This terror and temper had come about through a mistake in judgment on my part.

It all started when Mr. Cat learned to distinguish the particular ring of the bell which announced the arrival of his veterinarian, Dr. Louis J. Camuti, who loves cats and is the author of a delightful memoir called *Park Avenue Vet*. Because of secret knowledge possessed only by cats and some dogs, Mr. Cat always knew the doctor's ring, and would flee to some inaccessible part of the house. Therefore, half an hour before the doctor was due, I would place Mr. Cat's carrier beside my chair in the living room, gather him up and secure him in his valise. When the doctor was ready, I would open the carrier and produce the reluctant victim for the needle that would bring him back to health.

Though this procedure saved the doctor much time and all of us much trouble, it brought about a violent hatred in Mr. Cat for his carrier. He associated it in his mind with sharp needles, and hid when it was produced. It became necessary to keep the carrier strictly out of sight when a journey was imminent, and only produce it when the suspicious feline had been lulled into a sense of false security, and all avenues of escape had been blocked.

Friday nights and Saturdays were freedom days at Fire Island, but Sundays were something else again. The battle of the carrier had to be fought and we both knew it. Mr. Cat could run at will until he had his breakfast on Sunday morning then out-of-doors was forbidden. Guards (guests they fondly thought they were) watched the doors because once a certain puss was out, the chances were he would not be back until after the last ferry boat had departed.

One Sunday afternoon an unwary guest let a slim feline past and the hunt was on in earnest. Guests and neighbors formed a posse to try to capture the fugitive. Mr. Cat's name echoed through all the surrounding woods and gardens while cellophane was crumpled to make that sound supposedly irresistible to His Nibs, but all was in vain. The sun sank lower in the sky and soon was almost resting on the Great South Bay and I could see the last ferry for the day approaching the wharf. An unbreakable appointment made it essential that I be at my desk at the Library at nine o'clock on Monday morning. Ed Burke generously offered to stay overnight and return with the missing one the next morning. We were sure Mr. Cat would show up for his dinner after the last boat had gone. It would mean they would have to catch the 6:45 A.M. ferry which has long been referred to as "The Bucket of Blood" bearing away as it does those whose weekend lasted too long.

Ed saw our guests and me off on the boat, and then started back to the cottage. On his way he stopped often to call and to peer under houses hoping to turn up the vagrant.

There was no sign of a cat. We had left the kitchen door propped open so that should Mr. Cat return while the house was empty, he could get inside. All other exits were locked, so that he couldn't get out again once that kitchen door was closed behind him. When Ed entered the living room, there in the center of the big round hassock sat Himself, bright-eyed and bushy tailed, with an expression on his face that seemed to say, "Well, where have you been? It's dinner time, you know."

Charlie, the Dandie Dinmont.

7

A PERSIAN COMES TO CALL

Mr. Cat left us in January of 1960, and friends entered both sides of the discussion about obtaining another pet. Some were of the school which favors a new kitten being ensconced immediately. They believe that caring for and winning the friendship of a newcomer lessens the great sense of loss. The other school felt as I did that, since Mr. Cat had been more than a pet and so exceptional, it was too much for any kitten to try to follow in his footsteps right away. I knew that the gap would never be filled, and that eventually there would have to be another cat. However, knowing the ways of animals, I decided to let fate and time bring the answer, and would make no decision until the Fall. Ed agreed to this, remarking that for one summer at least he would be free to carry luggage in both hands. Every weekend from April to October for many years he had commuted with one hand inevitably attached to a cat carrier.

With no cat holding the cottage as his very own inviolable

territory, we were able to invite as guests those friends who had dogs to be included in the invitation. The first of these was Polly Dick and Charlie, her Dandie Dinmont, who had had such a trying visit earlier.

After Polly had installed herself in the guest room, Charlie frisked about, exploring the rest of the house, and all the deck which runs completely around the house, and all the bushes and trees around the deck. He had a dog yummy while we sipped our cocktails in the twilight, before traversing the narrow boardwalks to Pat's Ocean View Restaurant for dinner. Charlie had to be left behind, since dogs are *anima non grata* at Pat's.

Dinner was a prolonged affair and when we left the restaurant Polly hurried on ahead to release Charlie for his pre-bedtime walk. As cat people, this was a chore that Ed and I could act very superior about so we elected to enjoy the long way back to the cottage. We passed the tree-lined hollow on the bay side of Pride House and turned the corner of Prejudice Cottage. As we did, we sensed, rather than saw, a small dark shadow moving just ahead of us. Polly had taken our flashlight with her, so in the darkness we couldn't be sure what it was. Then we heard whatever it was jump off the boardwalk ahead of us and, after we had taken a few steps forward, jump up behind us. "It's a pussy cat," said Ed, reaching for the shadow which scooted ahead in true feline fashion and stopped at the corner. As we caught up, the lights from our house shone out on the walk to reveal our companion to be a handsome Persian who trotted right up the front walk with us and straight into the house when we opened the front door. Fortunately Charlie was still out on his walk with Polly, so our visitor was undisturbed. In the lamplight we could see our caller to be a beautifully proportioned Blue Persian with handsome and eloquent copper-colored eyes which were definitely asking for a handout as it wound back and forth between our legs with loud purrs.

"We have no real cat food," I said to the visitor, "but how would a saucer of milk do as a snack?" Ed proceeded to the kitchen and set down a bowl. The caller fell to the milk with dispatch. Ed returned to the living room to observe that the cat seemed terribly hungry. In no time at all, the Persian was back in the living room to settle down for a good wash.

It was then that Ed recognized the visitor. "This is Onni Saari's cat," he said. "You remember. Last Spring at the railroad station we saw him with a cat carrier for the first time. I asked him about his new pet, and he showed us this one. I remember her wonderful eyes."

The washing up completed, our caller sauntered over to the front door and asked to be let out. Ed obliged and we watched the plume of her tail disappear into the darkness.

I decided not to wait up for Polly and Charlie to return but headed for bed. Ed went next door to our neighbors, so our guests returned to an empty living room. Finding no one to talk to, they proceeded to their own room and settled down for the night.

Ed decided to go on with our neighbors to a late party, and came back to our cottage to leave word. As he opened the front door, the Blue Persian suddenly jumped out from the bushes and came in with him. When Ed saw that everyone was in bed, he cautioned the cat about sleeping dogs and put down another saucer of milk. When she finished, they both left to go their separate ways.

As Ed was returning home, a sudden summer storm broke, and he ran the last part of the way through heavy rain. When he reached the front door, he found a huddled mass of wet blue fur crouched on the sill. He brought in our three-time visitor and towelled her until her fur shone and her purrs were threatening to wake up the entire house. He was a little chagrined that there still was nothing more than milk to offer, but that was downed with such relish there could be no doubt it was most welcome.

The downpour had not lessened, so Ed decided our visitor should become an overnight guest. The Persian sat in the doorway to his bedroom and watched him prepare for bed with her enormous orange eyes. As he reached to turn out the light, he patted the bed at his side, and the cat jumped up and snuggled down to sleep. As Ed said later, it was good to have a cat under the roof again.

About five o'clock the next morning in the false dawn, Polly was awakened by violent shaking of her bed. The sturdy Charlie was standing at the foot, vibrating with excitement, and getting ready to spring to the floor. Looking around for the reason for his agitation, Polly was amazed to see a sedate Persian cat staring serenely back at Charlie with large and expressive eyes. "Shoo," said Polly, waving her arm. "Go away. I don't know how you got here, but go away." To her great relief and Charlie's great disappointment, the cat did go away.

Her next appearance was at five fifteen when I was suddenly shocked from a sound sleep by a large thump on my stomach. My eyes flew open to see the Persian Blue with the large eyes standing stiff legged on my middle demanding in no uncertain meows to be let out. Since my bedroom has its own outside exit, I was selected to be doorman. I got out of bed to oblige her wondering just how she had got in again. I was too sleepy to puzzle it out and returned to my bed, after watching the Persian pause momentarily in the doorway for a minute then depart with a flip of her tail.

Around nine o'clock Polly appeared in the living room to find me seated there, and her first question was, "Where did that cat come from?" Then she told me of her surprise at dawn. I countered with my own tale of surprise, and filled her in on the details of the earlier encounter, but this still did not explain how the cat got back in. Ed, having been awakened by our conversation then put in an appearance and explained the whole sequence. Both Polly and I suspected he would have kept the cat with him even if the night had been fair and not stormy.

Charlie, meanwhile, had been doing his Dandie Dinmont best to sniff out all traces of his nocturnal vision. As we all adjourned to the kitchen to prepare breakfast, he scooted past us into my bedroom to sniff and snuffle at the door out of which our visitor had made her last exit. "Pussy cat is gone," said Polly. She swung the door open to show him that his search was in vain and there sat the Persian! "Oh, no!" we cried as one while Charlie wriggled in glee. We explained to our persistent visitor that the nighttime emergency was over, and that she

The sturdy Charlie greets a Persian.

had a perfectly good home of her own. It was time she went to it. At that to our amazement, she turned, and once again we viewed her waving plume as it followed her down the board-walk.

For cat lovers who were catless, it had been a most delight-ful interlude.

8

A PERSIAN COMES TO STAY

The next weekend I was sitting on the side deck of *St. George and the Dragon,* when Ed appeared from one of his frequent expeditions with a puzzled expression on his face.

"I just ran into Onni Saari," he began, "and I told him about our taking in his cat last Saturday night. He said he was so grateful because he had been called away, and then, after I finished raving about the cat, and told him how much you admired her, out of a clear sky he said, 'Do you want her? I'll give her to you.' I was so surprised I didn't know what to say. I said I'd talk to you and tell him later. What do you think?"

I was as astonished as Ed. The nocturnal visit had been pleasant but I had never considered the guest as a permanent boarder. Although there had been vague talk about acquiring another cat, it had all been projected into the future. Any plans had concerned a kitten, as Mr. Cat had been when we first met, a ball of fluff to train, teach and develop. Our visitor was a fully developed cat with a personality of her own and with a decided will. Then I reminded Ed that he had been the one to welcome a summer *sans* cat-carrier. But I could tell that the caller had completely defeated that defense, and Ed only needed one word from me to run and fetch the Blue Persian home.

We let the matter rest for that day, but discussed it often during the following week. Finally a compromise was reached. We would accept Onni's gift if later on we could find a kitten to join the household. Ed could hardly wait to get off the boat the next Friday to find Onni and collect the cat.

He arrived back completely dejected. Onni had changed his mind and felt he just couldn't part with his pet. I felt terribly depressed, too. Having been slightly reluctant about acquiring a grown cat, I had reasoned myself into accepting the Persian Blue. I recalled all the sweetness and beauty she displayed on her first visit, and now I felt I had lost a companion without ever having known the cat.

The following Friday night as we were finishing dinner in Pat's Restaurant on the Island, we spied Onni rushing to our table. He threw himself down in a chair and exclaimed, "If you still want the cat, come with me now. I've been away and I haven't seen her. If I go back and pick her up, I'll be lost again and can't do it. Come right now and take her away." Ed flew out of the restaurant on Onni's heels while I went back to *St. George and the Dragon*. Soon Ed was at the door with a shiny black carrier which he opened. The beautiful Blue Persian rose and stretched, lifted the most expressive amber eyes you ever saw and then descended from her chariot. She sniffed fingers, and then began a slow tour and inspection of her new home. We wondered if she remembered her visit of three weeks before. We sat very quietly in the living room until she returned from her tour. She sat down to wash, apparently pleased with her new domain and lifted her lovely eyes. That settled it. I knew what her name was to be. Amber, Mistress Amber, as opposed to Mr. Cat and as abundantly appropriate.

Amber was then and is now a beautifully proportioned cat, square and chunky. As I observed her at length, and watched as she enjoyed her first meal with us, and then inspect the pan which had been fixed for her, I suddenly suspected pregnancy. Everyone knows that a smart and sensible cat makes good preparation far in advance for an oncoming family. Had this been the reason for the late night pick-up on the board-walk? Ed concurred in my analysis, but thought we should seek more expert advice before assuming anything.

In the morning, we asked our next door neighbors in to meet and admire the new member of the household. Marion Leighton, who is a practicing veterinarian, praised Amber extravagantly, which pleased both Amber and me, and then I casually asked Marion's opinion about motherhood. "Well," she said, "It's hard to tell, at least at this stage. She could be just a plump cat. I wouldn't want to say."

We asked Onni if he had any idea, saying first, that we were not making this a qualification of acceptance. According to the papers Onni gave with Amber, she was just over a year old, and romance could have occurred easily under a summer moon in the beautiful tree-lined garden of Onni's house. He admitted it could easily have taken place, since he had been away so much.

When we returned to town on Sunday night, Amber came along to spend her first days at 19 East 55th Street. She settled right into the apartment without a qualm and made herself at home. When Dr. Camuti called to begin her anti-enteritis shots, I asked the additional and now all important question as to whether or not Amber was in the family way. Again the professional refused to commit himself. After he had departed I looked at Amber and then at Ed, "I don't care what they say," I said, "That cat's pregnant. She knows it and I know it." And as the weeks went by Amber's burgeoning gave growing testimony to the truth.

The next weekend we returned to the Island again with Ed back in harness with a cat carrier. He accepted cheerfully the laughs and jeers of those who had heard his resolve to spend one summer at least detached from this piece of luggage. The first week end she spent at *St. George and the Dragon* we had not let her out, and after her previous outdoor existence she had not seemed to mind at all. However, after a week in the New York apartment, the outdoors seemed very attractive and we heard once more the insistent demands at the door for "Out" and "In."

On Saturday morning as I sat enjoying the sun on the deck, Onni suddenly appeared with Amber. "She came back," he said. "I was painting an upstairs window and looked down from the ladder and there she sat. So I brought her back." I asked Onni to put her in the house, which he did and departed. Amber proceeded straight through the house to the kitchen where she found Ed and demanded to be let out the back door. He complied and thought no more about it.

Fifteen minutes later Onni was back again and Amber with him. The same scene was enacted, and Ed again let her out the back door, wondering how she had got back in each time.

By the time Onni returned the third time, looking very harrassed, I had brought Ed up to date on all occurrences. He looked at Onni and said slowly, "Tell me, have you been up on the ladder each time Amber had appeared, and have you put down the brush and put down the paint and come all the way down the ladder to get her and then bring her all the way back here?"

"Yes," said Onni.

"Well," I said, "It's time you learned about cats and their sense of humor. As long as you are willing to stop everything you're doing and make all this fuss, Amber will be over there everytime we let her out of the house. Next time she does this, which will be in about five minutes I imagine, ignore her. Don't pay any attention and she'll soon get bored. You'll see."

Looking skeptical about this theory, Onni returned to his painting and did not re-appear. Later that afternoon on my way back from the grocery store I passed by his house. Onni was now working on the downstairs windows. "Is Amber around?" I asked.

"She was," he answered, "but I haven't seen her for some time."

I raised my voice, "Amber. Mistress Amber. Are you around here?" There was a rustle under the boardwalk and then right at my feet up jumped a very pleased Persian. "Amber" I said, "Come home. It's almost dinner time, so stop this nonsense and come get fed." I started on my way and Amber trotted right along with me. Mr. Saari had learned another mysterious fact about cats.

When I had asked him earlier concerning her name, he had told me he had always called her "Kitty. Just Kitty," and when I had examined her papers I saw that the space for the cat's name was blank. But from that moment I first said, "Amber" she knew it was her name. I have never seen any cat who so approved of her name. From that first utterance she knew it was hers and has responded without hesitation ever since.

As the weeks progressed and Amber grew and grew in size, Ed and I read everything we could lay our hands on concerning cat accouchements. We tried to reckon the time, knowing that the gestation period is 63 days, but since we had no idea exactly when the mating took place, we could not fix a time. My vacation came round, and Amber and I settled in at the Island. Ed arranged his vacation so that we were sure that the denouement must take place during his two week span. Both of us having spent seventeen years with a neutered male cat were extremely apprehensive about the coming event. Amber was the only complacent one as she ate more and more and grew and grew. Our belief that we had approximated the right time was confirmed when Marion Leighton's husband upon spying Amber rolling down the boardwalk called out "Haven't you confined that cat yet?"

"Confined her?" I asked.

"Well," he responded, "Unless you want her to have them under the house and look forward to ripping up the floor boards to get at them, you'd better confine her. She looks almost due to me."

At that point the institution of the air-lock began. The front door was barred to all. Exit was made by going from the

Hurricane warnings.

kitchen to my back bedroom and closing the kitchen door. Then, and only after that door was closed, could the door to the deck be opened. On entering the procedure was reversed. At no time were both doors opened simultaneously.

Ed gathered a lot of old clean cloths and prepared nests in the backs of several closets, allowing Amber to inspect each one in turn. She inspected each one, and then walked away without a backward glance at any of them.

August raced towards September and the total time of Amber's adoption reached sixty days. There couldn't be more than three days left for we knew she had not been in season during the time she had been with us. Neighbors, friends, acquaintances, delivery men were constantly asking if the great event had happened. We had gone from cheerful acknowledgements of "Any day now" to monosyllabic denials. Ed's vacation was drawing to a close, and he took to racing up and down the living room with Amber hoping to start something up. But Amber just played happily, stopping only to go to the kitchen for another meal. From the amount of food she was consuming and the size she had swelled to, I was predicting a fabulous birth of twenty kittens at one time.

Labor Day passed, and even the constant dinning of that day's name into her ears did nothing for Amber. Ed had to return to town, leaving me slightly apprehensive and Amber thoroughly complacent.

That Sunday night, the first we were alone, hurricane warnings began to sound over the radio. Around eleven o'clock Amber and I repaired to bed for what was to be mostly a sleepless night. At what seemed about ten minute intervals someone would stomp up the deck to shout in my bedroom door that most people were evacuating because of the oncoming storm and offering kind service in assisting me and Amber to the dock.

Since my illness I have walked with a cane and my balance on uneven boardwalks is precarious. The winds had reached the velocity of sixty miles an hour, and I was more apprehensive about the walk to the dock under such conditions in the dark than what the storm could do. I also felt that a heaving journey across the Great South Bay on a small ferry boat might accomplish for Amber what Ed's exercises had not brought about. I kept rejecting the proffered help with thanks. I did know that my next door neighbors were still in residence, and that kept up my morale.

Then I heard *them* call over to me. They had grown increasingly nervous what with all the warnings and departures and had decided to leave for the mainland. I stuck by my decision to remain, but I wondered if I had really done the right thing. The sound of people on their way to the dock kept me awake as much as did the ever increasing sound of the storm itself. I felt really alone and was glad that Amber felt like snuggling herself to me. The warmth from her furry body was a comfort in the night. I was reminded of the time Mr. Cat and I underwent the most violent of the 1954 hurricanes, but even that had been in the daytime. The pitch dark does make a difference in morale.

I was still trying to get to sleep and become as relaxed as Amber had now become, when once again I heard someone banging on my door. It was Onni with the news that the positively last boat would leave in half an hour, and that he would make sure that both Amber and I would get there.

At that point spirits were low. It was about half past four as I started to dress and steel myself for the imminent ordeal. Then I thought to ask Onni if he were going to accompany us all the way to the mainland, but he said, "No," he was going to remain. Sensing my great reluctance to leave, he volunteered to stay with Amber and me for the remainder of the storm which still had not struck with its full fury. He went off to his house to collect his own radio as my batteries were running low, and his barometer. Amber and I proceeded to the living room to light lamps and await his return. We then all settled down to listen to the gloom and doom pour out of the radio and watched the barometer fall lower and lower while the winds outside got higher and higher.

Drenching rains heralded the storm and I prepared a

large pot of coffee to cheer up Onni and myself. I gave Amber her breakfast hoping to decrease her nervousness, but though she ate heartily, she was obviously still tense.

Then came the six hour wait before the hurricane really hit. The winds and rain lashed the house and Amber paced the floor. Suddenly the barometer was lower than I have ever seen it, before or since. Amber got closer to me and we all prepared for the storm to strike. Though none of us had been present, we remembered how the ocean had broken through the dunes in 1938 and washed houses into the Great South Bay. I also remembered how the low barometric pressure always increases the activity in the maternity and lying-in wards of hospitals, but this must only apply to lady humans for Amber was just plain scared.

There was no doubt when the full force of the hurricane hit us. The winds rose to a scream and the house shook in the blasts of more than gale force. The windows rattled and banged and the rain smashed down, but everything held tight. After nearly an hour of incessant pounding, the lull which denotes the center of the eye of the hurricane arrived. Onni went out to survey the damage and inspect his property, but I warned him to return quickly as the storm would resume. Amber knew it would, too, for she did not relax for a minute all during the respite. It did return as did our friend with his reports of damage and survival. Since the wind had struck across the bay rather than from the ocean, the dunes had held magnificently. There was a good chance they would survive and so would we. We did.

A phone call from Ed late in the afternoon put his mind at rest that Amber was still expecting and not even a hurricane had loosed her brood. It was not until three evenings later when on returning from dinner, I discovered that Amber had decided now was the time and the place—the kitchen floor. Ignoring all the carefully prepared nests, she had decided that this event was not one for dark corners, but right out in the open.

Terry Wilson, a neighbor, dropped by to see if there were

news, and discovered Amber lying there with her litter of four. He carefully moved the brood to the bottom section of one of the kitchen cabinets, flush with the floor, lined with the soft cloths Ed had gathered. Amber obviously approved of the move for she settled down to wash each one thoroughly, and blinked at us serenely with her enormous amber eyes as the kittens settled down to nourish themselves.

That next weekend a constant parade of callers passed through our doors all eager to see what Amber had produced that not even a hurricane could shake loose. Though she was a full-blooded pedigreed Persian with champion bloodlines, Amber was not the least bit concerned that her offspring were four little black short-hairs. Two were supplied with snow white mittens and socks, the third sported a white spot right on the tip of its nose and the fourth was solid black. Amber was gracious about the kittens being picked up, though neither she nor I encouraged it. Humans are too careless and kittens are very wriggly. I doubt that the thought of germs entered her cat mind, but each kitten on its replacement was given a thorough bath from nose to tail tip after human handling. As I sat admiring the family, Ed reminded me how I had half held out against Amber for a kitten. "A kitten," he said, "Now you've got Amber and *four!*"

9

WHAT I KNOW ABOUT CATS

The question of how to bring up a cat successfully has plagued you and me and millions of others since the domestication of the cat though it hasn't bothered a single cat for a single minute. To a certain extent cats tend to bring themselves up provided their mothers are present and on duty. Humans can help with the weaning and thus provide themselves many amusing moments as they teach kittens to drink milk from a saucer and to enjoy their first taste of real beef. In the home mother cats have a tendency to let their kittens nurse for as long as they want. In their wild state the young would have left the lair before their mother became too debilitated from constant nursing.

It never takes long for kittens to discover the purpose of the sanitary tray and it is uproarious to watch a five weeks old bundle of fluff struggle up the side of his carton bed, precipitate himself to the floor, waddle to the tray, scramble up its side and then proceed to perform the necessary function, followed by wild and frantic scratchings flinging litter to the four winds. Having been washed by its mother at least fourteen times a day until one wonders if she isn't trying to turn the infant inside out, a kitten begins naturally to wash himself, his siblings, his mother and you if you are nearby when the washing mood strikes. This habit of fastitidous cleanliness will persist all its life. However, you can help with frequent brushings and grooming. This is most necessary if you have chosen a long-hair cat as your pet. Not only does it cut down on the number of hair balls which form inside your friend, but it prevents horrible snarls and tangles which lead to knots and mats of hair which must be cut away. It is never too early to get a kitten used to a brush, though at first it is a battle. It's all a fascinating game as far as a kitten is·concerned, but soon the idea gets across that this is an aid to grooming, and the unabashed vanity that is part of any good cat's personality leads him to welcome the combing and brushing and to complain if it is skipped.

If not done regularly there will be trouble when the comb hits a snarl, and the tugging begins. This hurts and you will hear about it in no uncertain screeches. One cat I know who lives on Gramercy Park has to be shaved regularly because his grooming did not start until too late and the mere sight of a comb causes him to throw an apoplectic fit which reduces his whole household to quivering lumps of flesh.

Cats should not be picked up unless they indicate they wish to be taken in your arms. They are not stuffed playthings to be carried about. The exception of course is on your arrival home after a short or long absence. Arrivals and departures are very important events in a cat's day. Seeing you leave, he wonders how you can abandon him even for a short while and his joy on your return is rapturous. That is the moment to pick up the happy animal and hear the purr factory go into high speed production.

Mr. Cat was always at the door to greet me, and Amber now has the same habit. After my illness, it was awkward for me to scoop up Mr. Cat with one arm, but between us we managed, and he would scramble up to my chest with his front paws on my shoulder. In fact, he had always rather liked that position and frequently had squirmed around and climbed my shoulder of his own accord. He then enjoyed having his bottom gently spanked. He showed his pleasure by increasing the rumble of his purr and kneading with his front paws.

Amber, on the other hand, likes to be picked up for only a moment on arrival, but likes more attention from time to time. She will suddenly appear by my side, and, as I put my hand down, she will rise on her back paws to meet me halfway. This is a great treat for both of us, but she does not like to be stroked under the chin as most cats do. The rule is, of course, to study your cat· and discover his likes and dislikes in the handling department. They soon make their wishes perfectly apparent. Madame Foo, a black Siamese of my acquaintance, adores being raised from the floor slightly by her tail.

Above all, talk to your cat a great deal and you will discover that soon he will begin to talk back to you. He can tell by your tone of voice much of what you are saying and in return will tell you what has been happening at home while you were absent. He will move about the apartment to point out what he is driving at and if you listen attentively and encourage him, actually following him around if he desires, you will find that you are learning a lot of cat language. Your response will increase his confidence and you will find he will tell you even more. But, please, do not use "baby talk." Dogs may like it but cats abhor it. One English lady used deliberately to direct "baby talk" conversation towards Mr. Cat, taking pleasure in the look of absolute horror that would come over his face, before he turned his back on her and stalked from the room.

Amber also becomes full of conversation whenever she is involved in a mishap. Most cats I have known run and hide when they accidentally knock something over, both to avoid punishment and also to cover up their terrible embarrassment at having been so awkward. Amber, however, immediately begins howling for everyone to come and see the awful thing that has happened. Perhaps she believes calling attention to the trouble will divert suspicion from her just as the one who discovers the body in any good mystery story is never guilty.

A basket of his own should always be provided for a cat even though he rarely may make use of it, preferring empty grocery bags or cartons. These latter are just so much catnip for a cat, fun to jump into and out of, full of delightful new smells, and perfect for sharpening claws. It is much better for him to use empty cartons which will be thrown away than furniture. Amber went through a period of sharpening her claws on an 1840 Howard and Davis clock which stands in the living room. This required a skirt of newspaper being tied around the clock until she became bored with the whole idea. Now she rubs against the sharp corners of the antique, but never scratches it.

There are a number of patented preparations which you can spray on your furniture to prevent cats from scratching, they say. I have endured the smell of these preparations and have yet to discover a cat that will be put off by them. If you have a set of furniture covered in the last piece of *petit point* crafted by a now extinct cloistered tribe of Eskimos, shut off the room it is in or expect some clawing.

Some people now have their cats de-clawed. If you like your furniture more than your cat one should have this done. If your cat is strictly a house pet and is never allowed out, then he may not need the natural weapons provided for his protection. A dog who has once felt the slashing claws of an aroused feline will never attack again.

The question of neutering or spaying is another matter. No one in his right mind will live in an apartment with an unaltered male, or else he will not be in his right mind for long. Altering also will improve the disposition of a tom cat, but the sense of maleness and independence can still be preserved. The sweetness of the female can still be retained if she is spayed. Allowing your female to go through season after season with her calling unanswered is bad for her health as well as your sanity.

The altered cat does not have to lose his figure. Sensible and regular feeding can keep your cat in shape. Overfeeding will result in a fat cat. We have all met those sluggish great lumps of fur that blink stupidly from the depths of an arm-chair. These monsters merely reflect their owners' inability to cope with the simple problem of a regular and sensible diet for their pets.

Cats are meat eaters, a fact that has been drummed into my head by Ed Burke, who came to share my apartment shortly after Mr. Cat had taken up residence with me. Ed had grown up with cats and, since he could never bear to part with the kittens after a new litter had arrived, had once cared for a collection of thirteen cats. His parents finally rebelled and the brood was pared down to two after Ed walked his neighborhood for miles finding homes for the surplus mousers. It was when he found me feeding Mr. Cat string beans that Ed held forth on the length of a cat's intestines, or rather the lack of length, which makes vegetables extremely hard to digest. "A cat is a carnivore," lectured Ed, though I have always thought that a frightening term to apply to a little house pet. "Put down a bunch of parsley and a nice slice of raw beef and see for yourself which is gobbled up first." Ed did finally relent to the point of allowing the strained vegetables given to babies to be included once in a while in Mr. Cat's diet, but even then they had to be mixed with meat.

It is expensive, but handy, to keep a supply of the small jars of chopped meat for "juniors" on hand. They provide an easy to prepare and nutritious meal for any cat. The canned "cat foods" should be considered as dietary supplements and not as staples. Variety in the types of food offered your pet will keep up his interest in his meals. They should be the high points of his day, morning and evening. It is fun to discover your cat's favorite food. With Mr. Cat beef kidney reigned supreme, while Amber is ecstatic about bacon-flavored crackers. She discovered them during her pregnancy when she was eating everything in sight. One fell to the floor and Amber pounced on it, tried it, loved it and came back for more. Now during the evening hours when humans mix their martinis, Amber arrives for her "cocktails" but she has a limit which is imposed. Her figure must not be forgotten.

Back in Richmond Mother Kitty adored lettuce and tomato salad with a light French dressing. Chin Chin loved stuffed olives but not the unseeded variety packed in brine. Trouble did too. I suppose he simply picked that up with his hero worship of the older male.

The most important concern in raising a cat, however, is the selection of a good veterinarian. Don't wait until your cat is suddenly stricken with some ailment with which you cannot cope before starting out to discover a doctor. Choose him as carefully as you do your own doctor and follow his advice. To look at it practically, it is to his advantage to keep your cat healthy and happy into a good age and you can cooperate best by following the vet's instructions. There never has been any sense in paying good money for medical opinion and then not following it.

You will find many people willing to give advice concerning cats and again it is best to put their opinions to the test of common sense. There is the typical old wives' tale of cats sucking babies' breath which I discussed elsewhere. Another old wives' tale is in reality the application of common sense. I am speaking of the tradition of buttering a cat's paws when moving to a new home. Most cats when taken from their carriers after a journey are upset when they feel themselves surrounded by all sorts of dangers in unexplored territory. The natural reaction is to run and hide as quickly as possible. If there is an open door, out they go, not stopping in their flight until exhaustion brings them to a hiding place. When they have calmed down, it is almost impossible for them to find their way back. In their precipitous flight they have sighted no landmarks to point the return course. The result is one lost cat. However, if butter is put on his paws, generously, at the moment the cat is allowed out of his carrier, as he attempts flight he discovers the nasty mess (to him) on his feet. His natural fastidiousness comes into play and he stops to wash off the offensive material. By the time he has finished thoroughly removing the butter, he has sensed that there is no real danger in the new surroundings and he can afford to explore them slowly and cautiously, gradually widening the circle of exploration with escape routes and hiding places carefully noted. The new house has become a home.